PASSENGER CARS OF NEW ENGLAND

VOLUME I
BOSTON & MAINE

BY

ROBERT A. LILJESTRAND

&

DAVID R. SWEETLAND

All of the photographs in this book are available from...

Bob's Photo
37 Spring St.
Ansonia, CT 06401
1-203-734-6666

The Railroad Press

The Railroad Press
PO Box 444
Hanover, PA 17331-0444

The Railroad Press Publishers of:

TRP Magazine

1930's New England Steam Action: Worcester

Chessie System: Cumberland Action

ALCO Reference #1

ALCO's to Allentown

CF7 Locomotives

Copyright © 2000 by The Railroad Press. All rights reserved. No part of this book may be reproduced in part or whole, in any form or means whatsoever, without written permission from the publisher, except for brief quotations used in reviews.

Printed in the United States of America.

International Standard Book Number 0-9657709-6-6

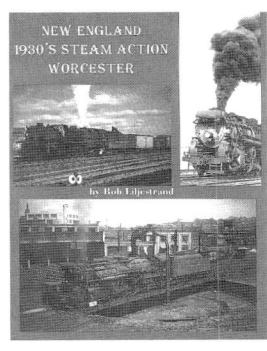

CONTENTS

Introduction 3	Combines 23
Wooden Coaches............................6	RPO-Baggage Cars 30
Gas-Electric Car Trailer 14	Baggage Cars 32
Gas-Electric Cars 16	Steel Coaches 34
Parlor Cars..................................18	RDC Cars 41
Dining Cars 20	Work Cars 42
Milk Cars 22	Index 48

DEDICATION

Tina Liljestrand

This book is dedicated to my wife, Tina, who has supported me thoroughly with the business.

ACKNOWLEDGEMENTS

This book is based on the collection of black and white negatives owned by Robert A. Liljestrand. Copies of the photographs can be obtained through Bob's Photo, 37 Spring Street, Ansonia, CT 06401. Text and captions were written by David R. Sweetland.

A special thanks to Harry A. Frye, Boston & Maine Railroad Historian, for technical assistance on Boston & Maine equipment and editing of the book. Harry Frye prepared the detailed B&M passenger car roster.
Also to Janet S. Watson for word-processing the text.

FRONT COVER PHOTOS: B&M Mountain #4113 with the EAST WIND. Boston & Maine R-1-d #4113 smartly moved the eleven-car EAST WIND by Barbers Crossing at Worcester, Massachusetts, in the summer of 1941. The cars were painted lemon-yellow, black roof, with a broad silver stripe. The inaugural eastbound run of the EAST WIND, Train #91, was made on June 21, 1940, using B&M Pacific #3712. Later R-1s with larger tenders would make the 148-mile run from Portland to Worcester to avoid a water stop. Trains #90 and 91 continued during the summers of 1941 and 1942 between Washington, D.C., and Bangor, Maine, for a total run of 706.6 miles in each direction. Two six-car train-sets were painted lemon-yellow in 1940 with more cars added later.
Photo by Norton Clark, collection of Bob's Photo.

Boston & Maine's RPO-Baggage car #3134 paused at Portland, Maine's Union Station on April 22, 1956. Built in 1914, number 3134 was part of the 3130-3137 group of RPO-Baggage cars. Photo by David R. Sweetland.

REAR COVER PHOTO: Pacific #3644 coupled to its train on July 3, 1954, before backing into Boston's North Station. This coachyard handled North Station's commuter trains as well as stored heavyweight Pullmans.
Photo by David R. Sweetland.

INTRODUCTION

Boston & Maine Passenger Equipment

During the 1940s and early 1950s, the Boston & Maine had one of the more interesting passenger car rosters in New England, everything from open-platform coaches to stainless-steel restaurant-lounge cars. All things would change rapidly with the delivery of RDC cars in 1952 and ending of most intercity services by the end of that decade.

In 1916, the Pullman Company delivered six, #4500 – 4505 (originally #1500 – 1505), steel intercity coaches to the B&M. These eighty-foot long coaches had a seating capacity for 88 passengers and rode on Commonwealth four-wheel trucks. At the same time Laconia Car Company built six all steel baggage cars, #2920 – 2925, also equipped with Commonwealth four-wheel trucks. Measuring sixty-four and one-half feet long, these baggage cars had a capacity of 20 tons and were renumbered #3200 – 3205 in 1923.

Built by the Pullman Company, seven all-steel parlor-buffet cars operated in B&M trains. Riding on six-wheel trucks, #20 MAPLE, #21 BIRCH, #22 ELM, #23 BEECH, #24 ONWARD, #25 PROGRESS and #26 HEMLOCK were later air-conditioned and in 1940 – 1941 moved to B&M ownership. They had a blind end at one end and vestibule at the other and rode on Commonwealth six-wheel trucks.

With the push towards more all-steel cars, the B&M took delivery from Osgood-Bradley Car Company of Worcester, Massachusetts, of five RPO-baggage combines in 1922 numbered 3110 – 3114. These cars had a thirty-foot RPO section and a baggage section with two sliding doors per side. These were followed by Osgood-Bradley coaches #4509 – 4580 in 1922 – 1923 some originally built numbered in the 4000 series as smokers. Osgood-Bradley also built in June and July 1923 eight, #3600 – 3607, baggage-smoking cars. Seating 48 in the smoking compartment, the car provided an over thirty-one foot baggage section. Each had vestibules at both ends and two sliding baggage doors per side.

One of the more unusual cars ordered during this period were six round-roofed RPO-baggage cars #3115 – 3121 with similar cars built for the NYC/B&A. In 1929 Osgood-Bradley completed these sixty-four foot long cars with Commonwealth trucks. The baggage section included two five-foot wide sliding doors per side and the RPO section one side door and three windows per side.

B&M obtained four all-steel dining cars, #84 MAINE, #85 NEW HAMPSHIRE, #86 VERMONT and #87 MASSACHUSETTS from the Pullman Company in December 1930. Seating capacity was thirty-six and the cars were ice-air-conditioned. A year later, the B&M purchased two baggage-smokers, #3608 and 3609 from Osgood-Bradley, a joint order with MEC's #521 and 522. These had roller bearing trucks and a single sliding door per side. Also jointly ordered were B&M coaches #4581 – 4584 and MEC #261 – 265 with a seating capacity of sixty-eight in "bucket" type seats and riding on four-wheel roller bearing trucks. B&M #4581 later became MEC #266 in February 1950 as a wreck replacement car.

On February 9, 1935, the streamlined FLYING YANKEE entered North Station, but didn't make its inaugural run until April 1. This Budd-built three-unit stainless-steel train was powered by a 600 hp Winton diesel engine for Boston – Portland – Bangor service. Also in 1935, Osgood-Bradley built B&M commuter coaches #1200 – 1220 as a start to replace the "splinter" fleet of open-platform coaches. That year's intercity event was ten Pullman-Standard, Osgood-Bradley built under lot W12512 "American Flyer" type coaches. Numbered #4585 – 4594, these eighty-five foot cars seated eighty-four in rotating seats and each car had a Frigidaire air-conditioning system. Two years later, twenty more (lot W6523), #4595 – 4614, were delivered, some equipped with roller-bearing trucks.

Starting in 1940, the Boston & Maine purchased used steel cars for commuter service. Pennsylvania

Railroad coaches became #800 – 899 and combines #3650 – 3656 and 3660 – 3665, followed by Delaware, Lackawanna & Western coaches to #901 – 925 in 1945 and Erie coaches to #950 – 969 in 1944. Reading steel coaches became #1400 – 1462 in 1946 and combines #3675 – 3696 the same year.

After World War II, the Boston & Maine and Maine Central jointly placed an order with Pullman-Standard's Osgood-Bradley plant for twenty-four modern stainless-steel passenger cars. B&M's part of the order was two restaurant-lounge cars, #70 BALD EAGLE and #71 HERMIT THRUSH, two combines, #3800 – 3801, and eight coaches (lot W6778), #4800 – 4807. Delivered in June and July 1947, the cars went into joint Boston – Portland – Bangor operation. Ten years later, the B&M sold the cars to the Wabash as the Boston & Maine was closing its intercity passenger business.

As the 1950s approached, the B&M went looking for more good steel cars on the used equipment market to replace its wooden fleet. C&O furnished ten six-wheel-truck cars, C&O #800 – 808, renumbered #4620 – 4628 and C&O #809 to #4425 in 1951 and at the same time twelve former round-roof NYC commuter cars became B&M #1225 – 1236. Standard NYC/P&LE coaches went to B&M #1300 – 1399 and P&LE/NYC combines became B&M #3618 – 3624 in 1953. In 1952, more Reading coaches became B&M #1463 – 1487 and combines #3671 – 3674.

In a joint order with the Bangor & Aroostook and New Haven, the B&M ordered in May 1953 from Pullman-Standard (lot W6942) four six-section, six-roomette, four double-bedroom sleeping cars, #31 HAMPTON BEACH, #32 OLD ORCHARD BEACH, #33 RYE BEACH and #34 SALISBURY BEACH. These stainless-steel cars were delivered in late 1954 – January 1955. In 1966, the B&M sold the four sleepers to the Canadian National after all Pullman-sleeper operations were closed.

Boston & Maine
Passenger Car Roster by Type

Steel Passenger Cars

Numbers	Former	Builder	Dates	Length	Notes	
			Suburban Coaches			
800 – 899	PRR	PSC	1910-3	64'5"	72 seat	acq. 1940
900 – 911	DL&W	BSC	1911	68'9½"	78 seat	901, 3, 7, 10 re# 60 – 63; some to Combines – re# 1945; 1951, re# 3625 – 41
912 – 925	DL&W	BSC	1914	68'9½"	78 seat	acq. 1945
950 – 969	Erie	SSC	1921	71'6½"	84 seat	acq. 1944
1200 – 1220		PS	1934	79'7½"	98 seat	
1225 – 1236	NYC	OBC	1923	79'6"	96 seat	acq. 1951
1300 – 1394	NYC	ACF	1926-30	78'9"	96 seat	acq. 1951
1395 – 1399	NYC	PS	1924	79'1¾"	84 seat	acq. 1951
1400 – 1462	RDG	BSC	1922-4	71'11½"	84 seat	acq. 1946
1463 – 1487	RDG	BSC	1922-4	71'11½"	84 seat	acq. 1952
1575 – 1599	1475 – 1499					orig. 800 series reblt. w/ generators, to 1500 series in '52 (from 800's to 1400's in '48)
			Combines (Coach – baggage)			
3600 – 3605		OBC	1923	80'3¾"	48 seat	2 doors 5'0"
3606 – 3607		OBC	1923	80'3¾"	46 seat	2 doors 5'0"
3608 – 3609		OBC	1931	81'5½"	44 seat	1 door 5'0"
3618 – 3624	ex NYC/P&LE 3618-19	PS	'25 & '21			
		SSC	1913	79'2"	48 seat	1 door 6'0" acq. '53
3625 – 3633	ex 900's ex DL&W	BSC	1911-14	68'9½"	42 seat	2 – 4'0" doors -rebuilt from coach '51
3634 – 3636	ex 900's ex DL&W	BSC	1911-14	68'9½"	58 seat	2 – 4'0" doors -rebuilt from coach '51
3637 – 3641	ex 900's ex DL&W	BSC	1911-14	68'9½"	58 seat	2 – 4'0" doors -rebuilt from coach '51
3650 – 3656	ex PRR	SSC	1910-11	64'½"	48 seat	1 – 5'5 3/8" door – acq. 1940
3660 – 3663	ex PRR	SSC	1915	64'½"	36 seat	1 – 5'5 3/8" door – acq. 1940
3664 – 3665	ex PRR	SSC	1912	64'½"	36 seat	1 – 5'5 3/8" door – acq. 1940
3671 – 3674	ex RDG	BSC	1923-5	71'11½"	56 seat	1 – 4'6" door – acq. 1952
3675 – 3696	ex RDG	BSC	1923-5	71'11½"		1 – 4'6" door – acq. 1946
3800 – 3801	"Purple Finch", "Blue Jay"	PS	1947	85'7"	44 seat	1 – 6'0" door

Numbers	Former	Builder	Dates	Length	Notes	
Coaches						
4000 – 4001	1532 – 1533	Pullman	1916	80'2"	seat 92	smokers
4010 – 4029		OBC	1923	80'1"	seat 92	some re no 4575 – 80
4400 – 4404	4510 – 4514	OBC	1922	80'1"	seat 74	partitions for smoking
4405 – 4406	4525, 4554	OBC	1922	80'1"	seat 74	partitions for smoking
4407	4552	OBC	1911	80'1"	seat 74	partitions for smoking
4425	C&O 809	St.LC	1935	79'10"	seat 68	partitions for smoking
4500 – 4505	1500 – 1505	Pullman	1916	80'1"	seat 88	
4509	4016	OBC	1923	80'1"	seat 92	
4510 – 4514 (1st)		OBC	1922	80'1"	seat 88	rebuilt to 4400 – 04 series
4510 – 4514 (2nd)	4000 series	OBC	1923	80'1"	seat 88	rebuilt from smokers
4515 – 4557		OBC	1922	80'1"	seat 84	
4558 – 4574		OBC	1922	80'1"	seat 88	
4575 – 4580	4024 – 4029	OBC	1923	80'1"	seat 88	
4581 – 4584		OBC	1931	82'4"	seat 68	4581 to MEC 266 – 5/1950
4585 – 4594		PS	1934	84'7½"	seat 84	
4595 – 4614		PS	1937	84'7½"	seat 84	
4620 – 4628	C&O 800 – 808	St.LC	1935	79'10"	seat 68	
*4800 – 4807		PS	1947	85'7"	seat 66	

*4800 – 4807 Car names: Bobolink, Robin, Hummingbird, Blackbird, Bluebird, Oriole, Chickadee, Snowbird

Numbers	Former	Builder	Dates	Length	Notes	
Mail						
3000 – 3001	2290 – 2291	B&S	1914	65'10"	rebuilt to MB 3130 – 3131	
3006	2292	B&S	1914	65'10"	rebuilt to MB 3136	
	2293	B&S	1914	65'10"	rebuilt to MB 2302, re 3100	
3007	2294, ex SC998	B&S	1914	65'10"	rebuilt to MB 3137	
3002 – 3003	2295 – 2296	B&S	1914	65'10"	rebuilt to MB 3231 – 3233	
	2297	B&S	1914	65'10"	rebuilt to MB 2303, re 3101	
3004 – 3005	2298 – 2299	B&S	1914	65'10"	rebuilt to MB 3134 – 3135	
3010 – 3015	2284 – 2289	LAC	1915	65'10"	rebuilt to MB 3012 to 3153	
3020 – 3021	2282 – 2283	OBC	1918	65'10"	3020 rebuilt to MB 3138, 3021 rebuilt to MB 3153	
Baggage – Mail						
3100 – 3101	2302 – 2303	B&S	1914	65'10"	1	4'0" door – rebuilt from mail cars
3110 – 3114		OBC	1922	64'0"	2	5'0" doors
3115 – 3121		OBC	1929	64'0"	2	5'0" doors – Arch roof
3130 – 3137	(see mail cars)	B&S	1914	65'10"	1	5'0" door – rebuilt from mail cars
3138	3020	OBC	1918	65'10"	2	5'0" doors – rebuilt from mail cars
3140 – 3142		OBC	1929	64'0"	2	5'0" doors – rebuilt to Baggage 3288-90 Arch roof (1955)
3150 – 3151	2300 – 2301	LAC	1916	74'0"	2	6'0" door – 3151 rebuilt w/Arch roof
3152	2283, 3021	OBC	1918	64'0"	1	rebuilt from mail car
3153	2286, 3012	LAC	1915	63'10"	1	rebuilt from mail car
3170 – 3173	PRR 5404, 08, 10, 11	SS	1916	64'5"	1	
3180 – 3182	Pullman 8135, 60, 94	PS	1944	54'8½"	1	ex-troop sleeper
Baggage						
3200 – 3205	2920 – 2925	LAC	1916	64'5"	2 – 8'0" doors (re no 1923) sold N de M 2/25/60	
3210 – 3213	2926 – 2929	OBC	1918	61'10"	2 – 8'0" doors	
*3225 – 3249	Pullman	PS	1946	54'8½"	1 – 7'0" doors – rebuilt from troop sleeper 1948	
*3260 – 3268	Pullman	PS	1943	54'8½"	2 – 6'8" doors – rebuilt from troop sleeper 1949	
*3269 – 3276	Pullman	PS	1944	54'8½"	2 – 6'8" doors – rebuilt from troop sleeper 1949	
3280 – 3281	C&O 403 – 404	St.L.	1930	76'11¼"	2 – 8'0" doors – acq. 1950, rebuilt from combine	
3285 – 3294 (1st)	Pullman	various		82'5½"	to 3300 – 3309	
3288 – 3290	3140 – 3142	OBC	1929	64'0"	2 doors 1 – 8'0" 1 – 6'0" rebuilt from MB 1955	
3291		B&S	1914	65'10"	2 – 8'0" doors rebuilt from MB 1955	
3292	85	Pullman	1930	84'2¼"	2 – 8'0" doors rebuilt from diner 1955	
3293	26	Pullman	1925	84'2¼"	2 – 8'0" doors rebuilt from parlor 1955	
3294 – 3295	20, 22	Pullman	1917	83'11½"	2 – 8'0" doors rebuilt from parlor 1955	
3296	23	Pullman	1911	82'11½"	2 – 8'0" doors rebuilt from parlor 1955	
3297	D&M 61	BSC	1930	74'3¾"	1 – 7'0" door, 1 – 8'0" door acq. 1953	
3298	86	Pullman	1930	84'2¼"	2 – 8'0" doors rebuilt from diner 1953	
*3300 – 09	Pullman	various		varies 84'2½"	2 – 8'0" doors – rebuilt from tourist slpr '54	
*3310 – 45	Pullman	various		varies 82'6½"	2 – 8'0" doors – rebuilt from sleeper 1954-6	

*ex Pullman was for 3225 – 49: 9762, 9766, 9771, 9776, 9780, 9288, 9791, 9801, 9805, 9818, 9823, 9833, 9849, 9851, 9862, 9868, 9877, 9916, 9925, 9929, 9956, 9966, 9978, 9989, 9997; 3260 – 79: 7251, 7335, 7453, 7473, 7476, 7511, 7562, 7590, 7611, 7832, 7889, 7891, 7906, 7915, 7950, 8036, 8059 Steel cars in 2200, 2300 & 2900 renumbered to 2900's, ca. 1922; 3100 – 01 rebuilt to Bag-Mail by 1922, 3130 – 38 after 1922; 3140 – 2, 3170 – 3, 3180 – 2 have 15' RPP, rest 30'; 2290 & 4 renumbered to VV10 and SC998, then 3006 – 7 ca. 1926, then 3136 – 7

* Pullman numbers for 3300 – 25: 1433, 2094, 2332, 2484, 1568, 2108, 2146, 2543, 2662, 1163, 2428, 1335, 1653, 1687 re 2544, 1760, 2062, 1074, 2428 re 1221, 2544 re 1687, 2059, 1293, 1571, 1961, 2088, 2092, 2586

* Pullman names/numbers for 3226 – 45: Fort Slocum, Fort Pickens, Peralta, Fort Treble, Milton, Monteagle, Butler University, Saoma, Greynook, 2091, 2095, 2622, 2650, Picacho, Martel, Shore Lark, Waldmeer, Wayneport, Sun Gold, Sun Light. Built various years from 1910 – 1930.

1. WOODEN COACHES

B&M Coach Interior. For the 1930s era commuter, this was the interior view of a 600 series open platform coach used in Boston commuter service. The rest rooms were located at opposite ends and lighting was supplied by a row of center overhead lights with power supplied by the generator on the steam locomotive. Walkover seats provided 2 – 2 seating in the overhead vented passenger section.

B&M #38, Coach. B&M coach #38 was photographed at Troy, New York, on April 19, 1936. Originally built as B&M #1038 by the Pullman Car Company, #1038 was renumbered to #38 in February 1930 and again to #518 in February 1937. This 91,100 pound coach had a seating capacity of 72 and measured 68' 1½" over couplers. Coaches #1037 – 1041 were all built in October 1906 and former #38 scrapped at Billerica Shops in May 1950.

B&M #80, Coach. B&M coaches #1077 – 1082 were built by the Pullman Car Company in June 1907. Car #1080 was renumbered to #80 in December 1930 and renumbered to #523 in December 1937. Photographed at Boston, North Station, on July 4, 1936, this 92,800 pound coach measured 68' 1½" over couplers and stood 10' 1" over top of rail. Former number 80 was scrapped at Billerica Shops in February 1948.

BOSTON & MAINE
132

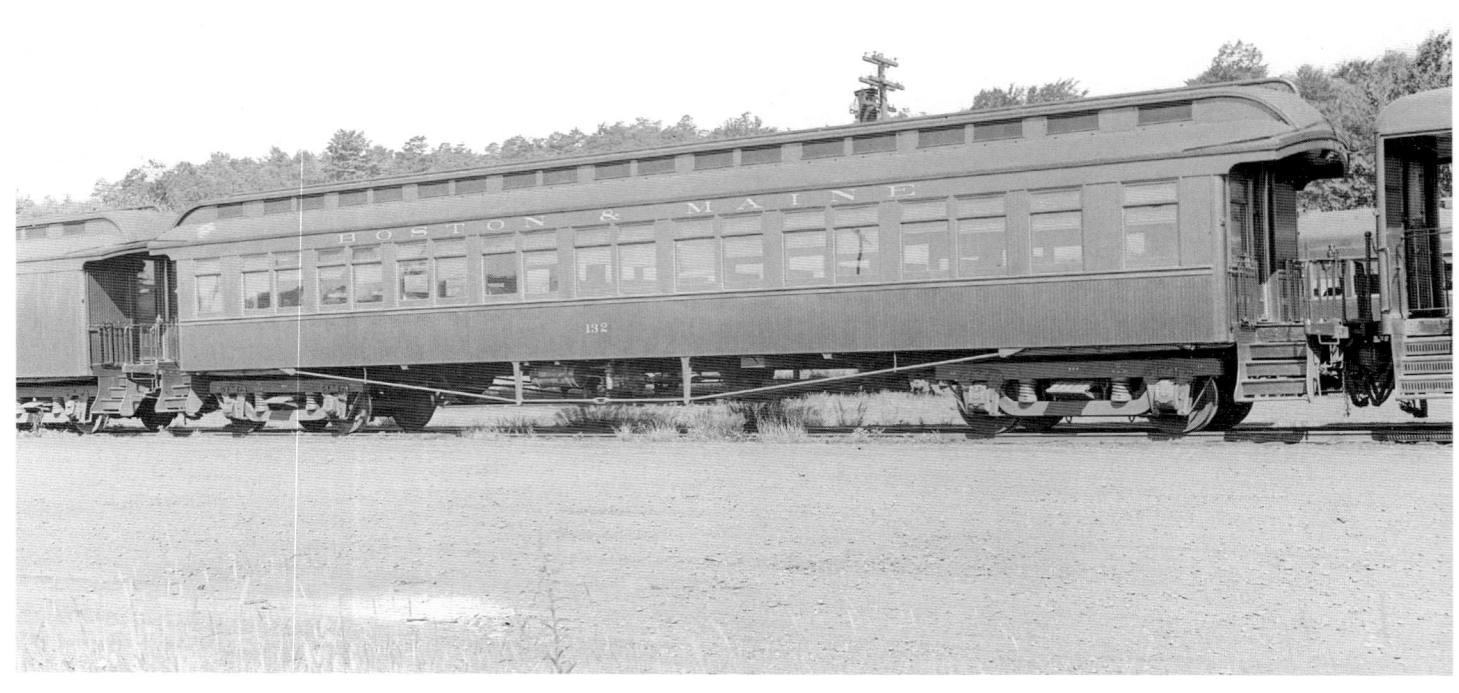

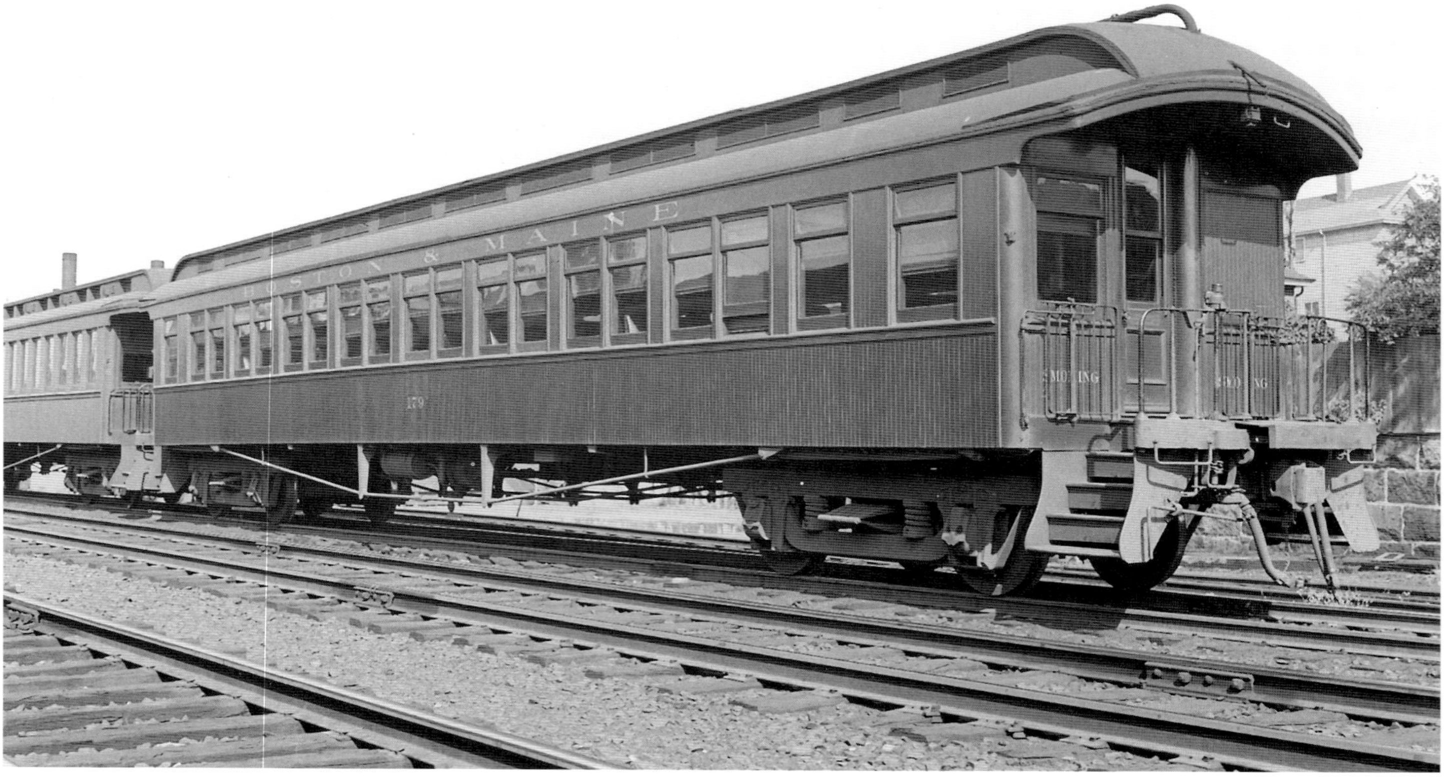
BOSTON & MAINE
179

B&M #132, Coach. B&M Coach #132 was originally numbered 847 then renumbered to #1132 and finally #132 in April 1931. Built by the Pullman Car Company in May 1896, #132 measured 68' 4" over couplers, weighed 86,200 pounds and seated 74 passengers. In June 1941 the car was changed to work train service and renumbered #W3249. This wooden car was retired and scrapped in May 1957. Photographed at Rockport, Massachusetts, on July 5, 1936, coach #132 operated in commuter service.

B&M #179, Coach. Built by the Pullman Car Company in August 1904, #179 originally came to the B&M as coach #1179. Renumbered in January 1932 to #179, the coach continued in passenger service until September 1948 when it entered work train service as #W3146. Retired in May 1962, it was sold to the Monadnock, Steamtown & Northern Railroad as their #146 in June 1962 and later in December 1968 sold to the Strasburg Railroad and named CHERRY CREST. When photographed at Lynn, Massachusetts, on July 4, 1936, it performed service as a smoker. The 66' 11" coach seated 74 passengers.

B&M #192, Coach. Coach #192 started on the B&M roster as #1192, built by the Pullman Car Company in July 1905. Coaches #1183 – 1185 and #1188 – 1197 were also delivered from Pullman at the same time. The 81,200 pound #1192 measured 68' 5" long and 10' 1" high and had a seating capacity of 72. Renumbered to #192 in January 1931, this coach remained in Boston and Maine commuter service until scrapped at Billerica Shops in August 1947. Number 192 was photographed at North Station Yard at Boston in May 1937.

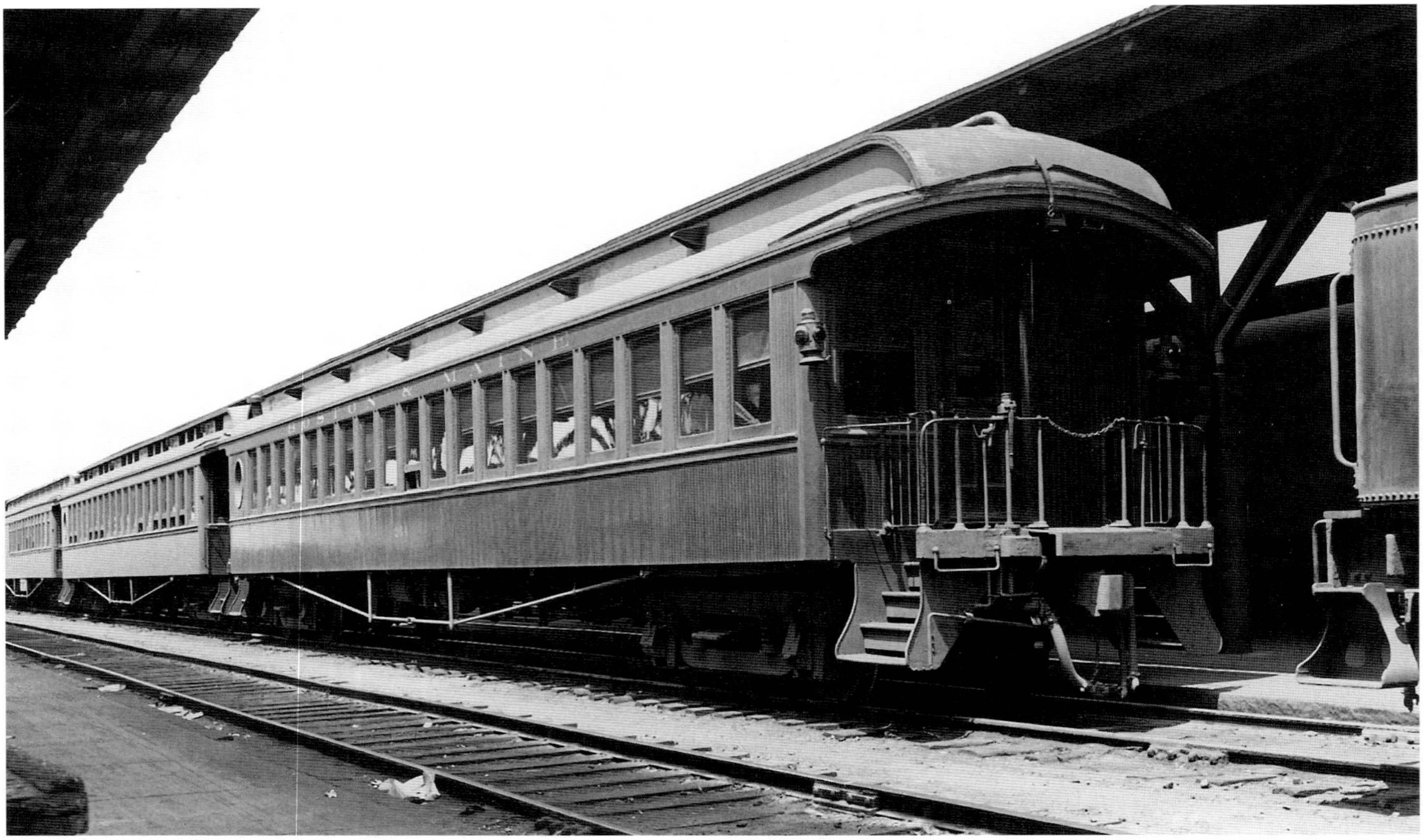

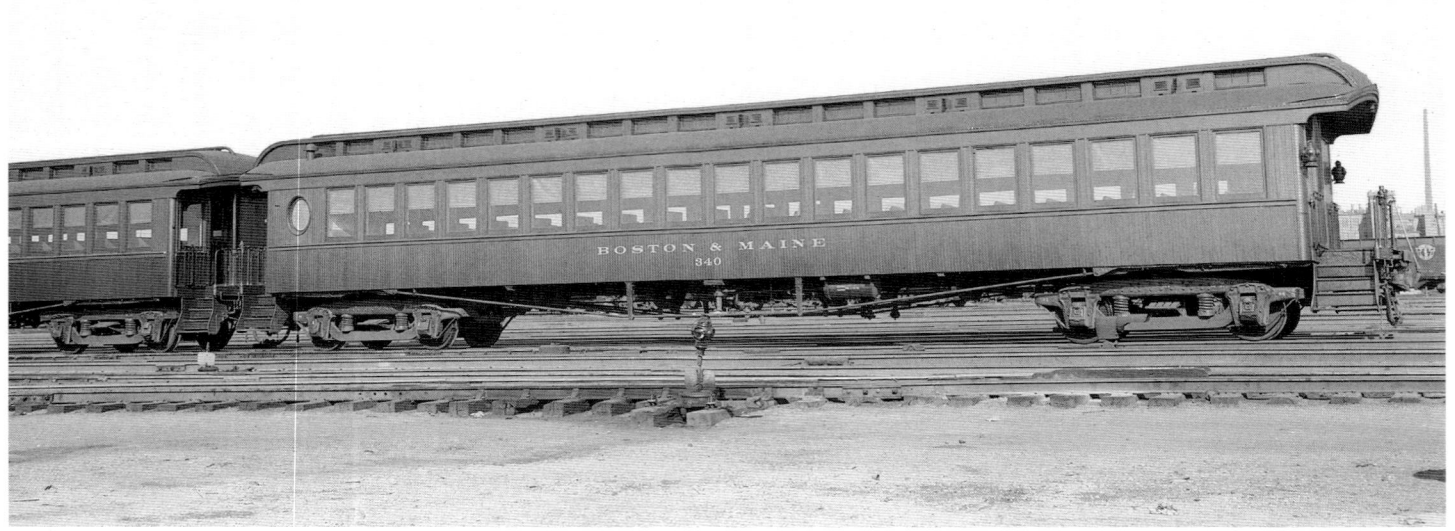

B&M #264, Coach. Open platform coach #264 was photographed at North Station in Boston on July 4, 1936. Originally built by the Fitchburg Railroad in 1884, #264 had seating for sixty-eight within its 60' 9½" long body. The wooden car had a steel underframe, truss rods and four-wheel drop-equalized trucks.

B&M #340, Coach. Laconia Car Company built B&M coach #1340 in September 1910. Other members of the group were B&M 1328 – 1424, all built in September and October 1910. Number 1340 was renumbered to #340 in May 1932 while in commuter service. These 68' 3" long cars (length over couplers) had a light weight of 90,000 pounds. Retired #340 was scrapped at Billerica Shops in October 1951. The major betterment for this coach was the application of a steel underframe sometime before September 1926.

B&M #445, Coach. Originally built by the Laconia Car Company in November 1911 as #1445, the coach was renumbered #445 in January 1931. Laconia built the #1425 – 1459 group of cars between October and November 1911. The open platform wooden cars were sixty-eight foot, five inches long over couplers and had a light weight of 77,700 pounds. B&M #1445 was retired in 1951 and then scrapped at Billerica Shops in December 1951. The car waited in the coach yard at East Somerville, Massachusetts, on April 28, 1946.

B&M #570, Coach. Built by Laconia Car Company in 1911, wooden coach #570 had vestibules at both ends with end glass windows. Renumbered from #1570 about 1930, #570 had seating for seventy-six and the car had an overall length of 68' 5". The car had a truss-rod underframe and rode on four-wheel, drop-equalized trucks. Coach #570's photograph was taken at Springfield, Massachusetts, on October 1, 1933.

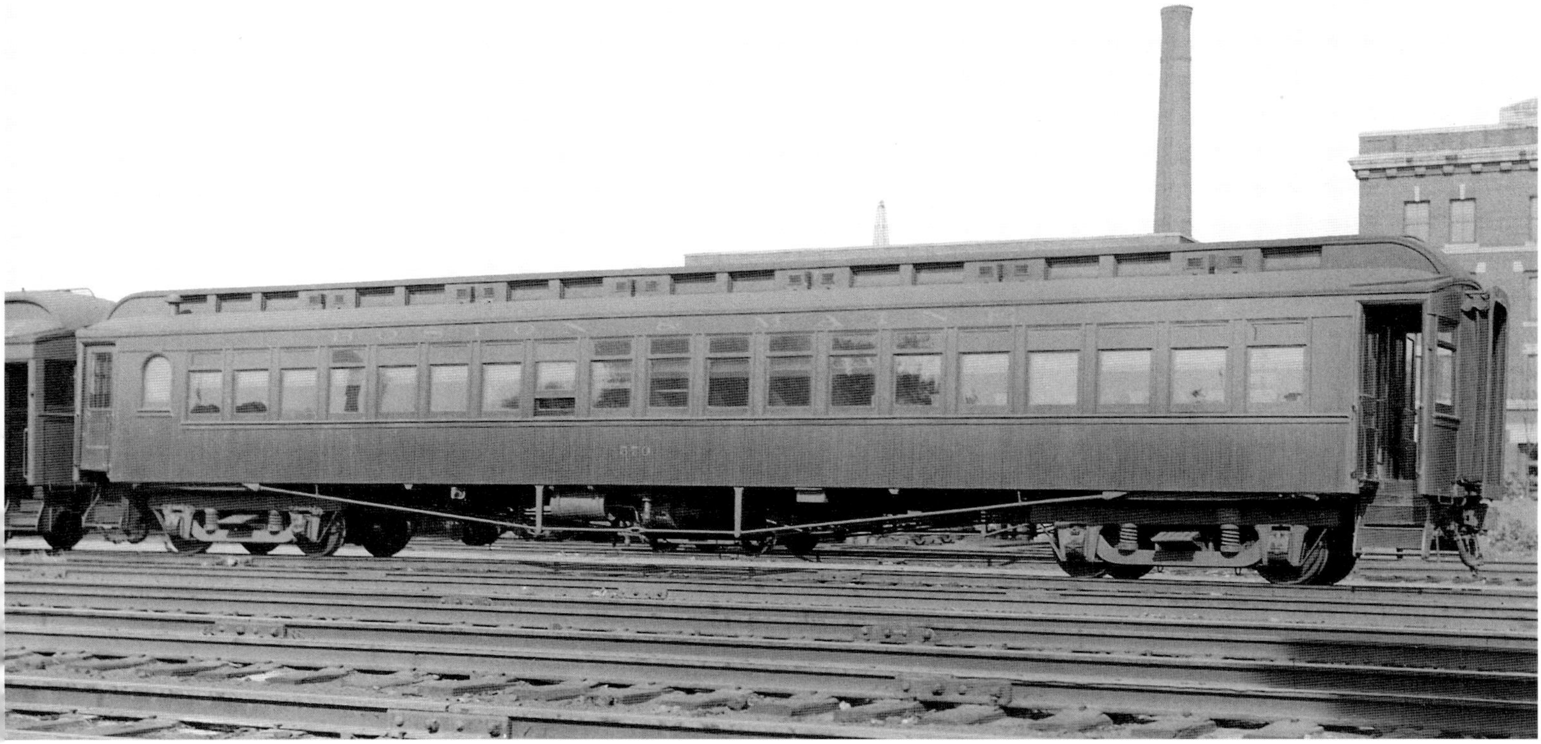

B&M #632, Coach. B&M #632 was built by the Osgood-Bradley Car Corporation of Worcester, Massachusetts, in April 1911. Number 632 continued in passenger service unit until scrapped at Billerica Shops in December 1951 after being replaced by newer steel commuter cars. The #600 – 665 series of cars were all built by Osgood-Bradley at the same time with similar dimensions, 68' 5" long and seating seventy-five. B&M #632 waited in front of the camera on October 30, 1948, at North Station.

B&M #671, Coach. Open platform coach #671 was built by the Osgood-Bradley Car Corporation in June 1911 seating 75 passengers. It measured 68' 5" long over couplers and had a lightweight of 88,600 pounds. Built by Bradley at the same time were coaches #667 –712. It remained in commuter service until October 1951 when it was retired and scrapped at Billerica Shops. The 671 was photographed at Reading Highlands on Aug. 1, 1936.

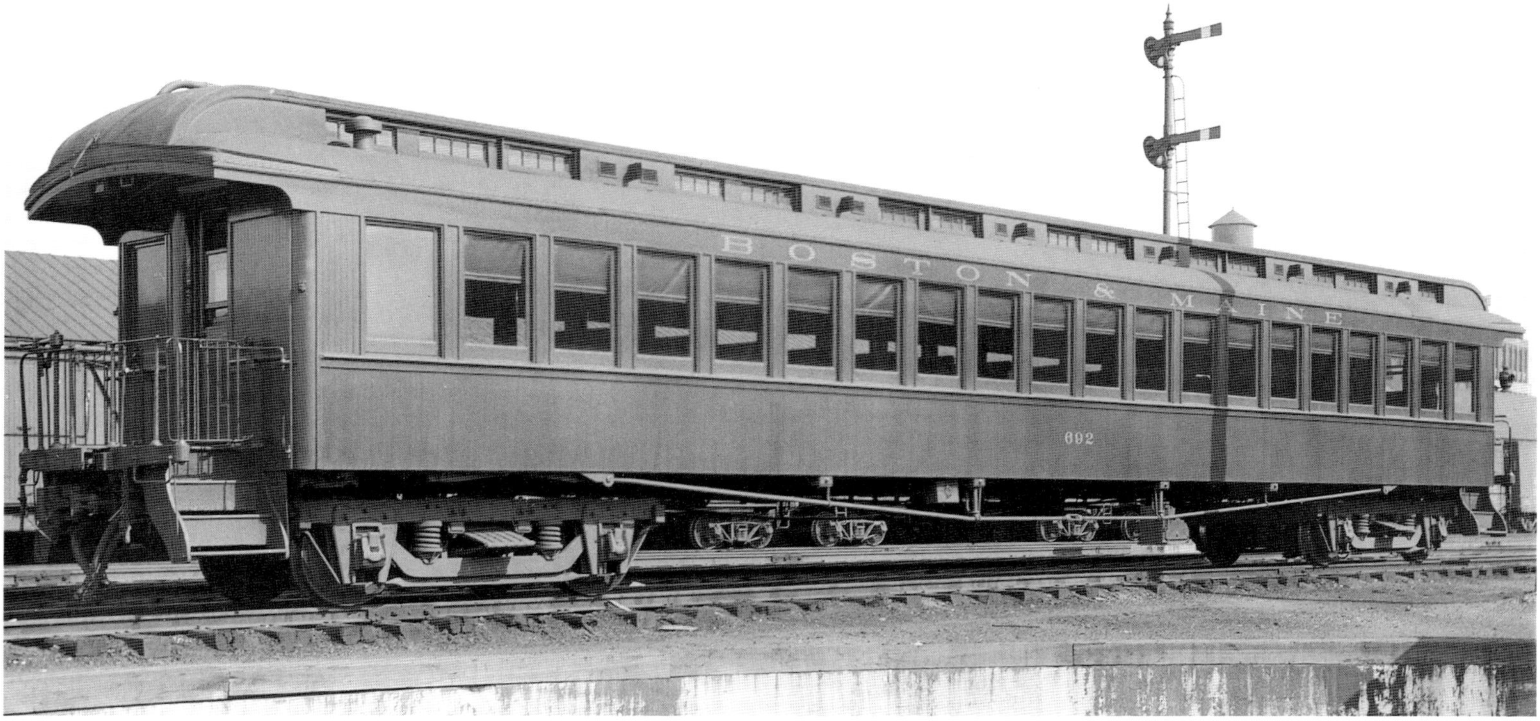

B&M #692, Coach. Boston & Maine open platform wooden coach #692 was built in July 1911 by Osgood-Bradley Carp Corporation measuring 68' 4½" over couplers. With a weight of 73,000 pounds, the coach seated seventy-five passengers and rode on four-wheel drop-equalized trucks. Number 692 was photographed at Springfield, Massachusetts, on October 1, 1933, before being retired and destroyed at Billerica Shops in September 1939.

B&M #699, Coach. Osgood-Bradley built coach #699, which arrived on the B&M roster in July 1911, seating 75. This 68' 5" long open-platform coach had a light weight of 88,600 pounds and had a truss-rod equipped underframe. The car continued in Boston commuter service until scrapped at Billerica Shops in April 1953. Number 699 was photographed at North Station on October 30, 1948.

2. GAS-ELECTRIC CAR TRAILER

B&M #1080, RPO-coach trailer. RPO-coach trailer #1080 was originally built for the Boston & Maine as #80 by the Brill Company in 1926. This all-steel 50' 10½" long car had seating for thirty-seven and a fifteen-foot mail section. Number 1080 was a trailer for a gas-electric car and rode on traction type four-wheel drop-equalized trucks. The trailer was photographed at Portsmouth, New Hampshire, on August 1, 1936.

Boston & Maine
Steel Motor Car Trailers

No.	Former		Builder	Date	Notes	
1060	White River RR	101	Laconia	1917	60'	38 seat Steam car
1070		70	Brill	1926	55'	73 seat Coach
1071		71	Brill	1926	55'	73 seat Coach
1080		80	Brill	1926	55'	37 seat Mail – coach
1081		81	Brill	1926	55'	37 seat Mail – coach
1090		90	Brill	1926	63'	93 seat Coach

3. GAS-ELECTRIC CARS

B&M #1180, Gas-electric. Osgood-Bradley built the B&M #180 – 187 group of EMC railcars in September 1926. With a length of sixty-one feet and weight of forty-seven tons, B&M #180, later renumbered 1180, was powered by a 275hp Winton engine. Boston & Maine #1180 and trailer stopped at Waltham Highlands, Massachusetts, in August 1937.

B&M #1182, Gas-electric. Electro-Motive Corporation built eight model 120 gas-electric cars at the Osgood-Bradley plant in September 1926. Originally numbered 180 – 187, the cars were sixty-one foot long and had a light weight of up to forty-eight tons. The cars were powered by a 275 hp Winton engine with GE electrical equipment and seated sixty-five in the passenger section. Number 1182 was photographed on the engineer's side at East Somerville, Massachusetts, on August 13, 1947. The car was renumbered 182 in June 1951 and retired in July 1955.

B&M #1187, Gas-electric. B&M #1187 and trailer were at Clinton, Massachusetts, on April 25, 1948. Viewed from the fireman's side, #1187 had a typical cooling arrangement for the 275 hp Winton engine. The baggage section had one sliding door on each side and each car rode on four-wheel drop-equalized trucks. Boston & Maine renumbered this gas-electric car to #187 in June 1951 and retired the car in June 1955.

4. PARLOR CARS

Boston & Maine
Steel Diner - Parlor - Observation - Pullman

No. & Name	Builder	Date	Notes
20 "Maple"	Pullman	1917	Buffet – Parlor 82'5", to baggage 3295 – 6/53, ret 12/59
21 "Birch"	Pullman	1917	Buffet – Parlor 82'11½", sold for scrap 3/15/57
22 "Elm"	Pullman	1917	Buffet – Parlor 82'11½", to baggage 32/4 – 3/55, ret 12/59
23 "Beech"	Pullman	1911	Parlor 82'11½", to baggage 3296 – 1952
24 "Onward"	Pullman	1914	Café – Parlor 85'9", sold for scrap 3/15/57
25 "Progress"	Pullman	1914	Café – Parlor 85'9", sold for scrap 3/15/57
26 "Hemlock"	Pullman	1925	Parlor 83'11½", to baggage 3293 – 1955
31 Hampton Beach	PS	1954	Sleeper 85'6", sold CNR 6/23/66
32 Old Orchard Beach	PS	1954	Sleeper 85'6", sold CNR 6/23/66
33 Rye Beach	PS	1954	Sleeper 85'6", sold CNR 6/23/66
34 Salisbury Beach	PS	1954	Sleeper 85'6", sold CNR 6/23/66
70 Bald Eagle	PS	1947	Restaurant-Lounge 85'7", sold Wabash 5/1957
71 Hermit Thrush	PS	1947	Restaurant-Lounge 85'7", sold Wabash 5/1957, later Buffet-Diner
84 Maine re: Mountaineer	Pullman	12/30	Diner-Lounge 84'9½", sold F.N.Blount 12/59
85 New Hampshire	Pullman	1930	Diner 84'9½", to baggage 3292 5/55, ret. 11/19/57
86 Vermont	Pullman	1930	Diner 84'9½", to baggage 3298 3/53, ret. 12/59
87 Massachusetts	Pullman	1930	Diner 84'9½", to insp. car 3333 – 12/50, re# 4444 1/55, ret. 11/66
95 (2nd) Mountaineer ex D&H 163	D&H	1932	Diner-Parlor 79'8¼", acq 12/9/1942 to W3154 – 3/1948, scrap 3/22/1956

B&M #4, Parlor. Parlor cars #1004 – 1007 were built by the Pullman Car Company in May 1907 for the B&M. These cars weighed 90,000 pounds and measured 68' 2" long over couplers. Numbers 1005 – 1007 seated 30 passengers in parlor seats and #1004 28 passengers. Car #1004 was renumbered #4 in June 1934 and renumbered to #501 February 1937. This car remained on the roster until 1952 when it was scrapped at Billerica Shops in February. The photographer managed to catch #4 on film at Boston on July 5, 1936, during the short time it carried that number.

B&M #515, Parlor. The Pullman Car Company built the #1004 – 1007 group of B&M parlor cars in May 1907. Parlor #515, former #1005, was sixty-eight feet, two inches long and had a light weight of 90,000 pounds. With seating for thirty, the closed vestibule wooden body rode on four-wheel trucks and had a truss-rod underframe. This parlor was renumbered to #5 in April 1930 and then to #515 in February 1937. Photographed at East Somerville, Massachusetts, on August 13, 1947, #515 continued in service until 1950.

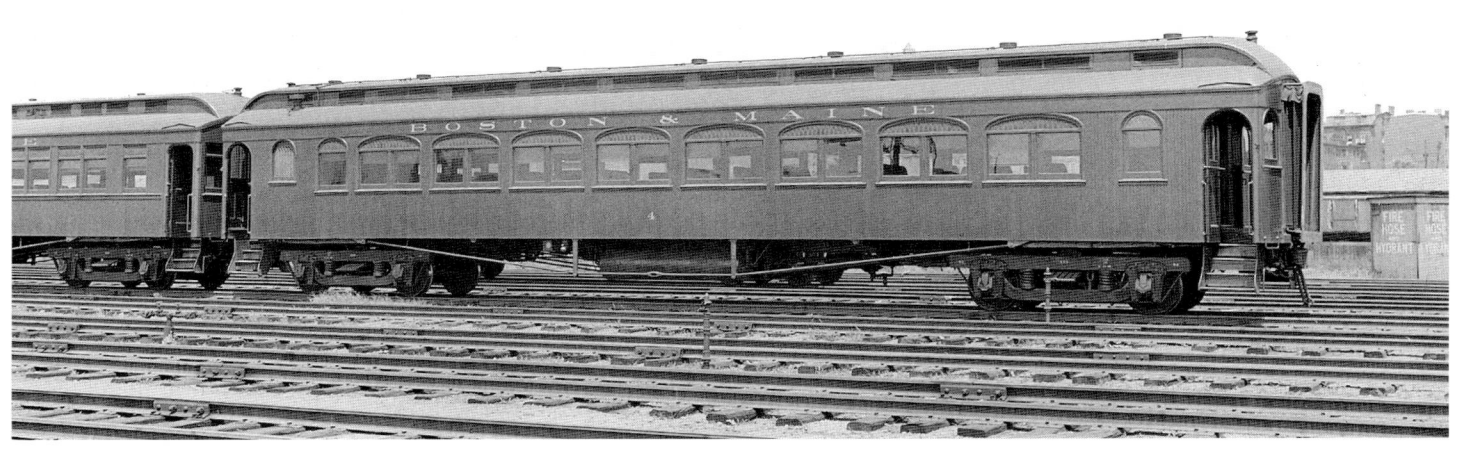

5. DINING CARS

Diner Interior. One of the #84 – 87 series all-steel diners was assigned to snow-train service in 1938. In the dining room, two waiters had finished serving passengers. Built by the Pullman Company in December 1930, the car was of all-steel construction and air-conditioned via the overhead vents. The over-window lighting was typical for Pullman cars of the 1930s.

B&M #87, MASSACHUSETTS Diner. The Pullman Company built in December 1930, four all-steel dining cars, #84 the MAINE, #85 the NEW HAMPSHIRE, #86 the VERMONT and #87 the MASSACHUSETTS. Each car has a length of 84' 9 ¼" over buffers and road on 6-wheel Commonwealth 5 x 9 trucks. The cars were air-conditioned and had a Vapor heating system. In December 1950, #87 was changed to Instruction Car #3333, renumbered 4444 in January 1955 and retired in November 1966. This beautiful heavyweight diner was photographed at Portland, Maine, on July 18, 1935.

#2222, Instruction Car, former Diner. Former B&M diner #1095 was built by Pullman Car Company in July 1906 in the group of diners #1094 – 1099. This 124,600 pound car measured 80" 7½" long and seated 28 in the café section. The steel underframes and wood sheathed diner rode on 6-wheel iron and wood trucks with 5 x 9 journals. Changed to an Air Brake Instruction Car in April 1926, the diner was renumbered #2222 and continued in that service until scrapped at B&M Billerica Shops in December 1950. Photographed at Boston on May 30, 1937, the car had been placed on a siding for air brake classes.

6. MILK CARS

B&M #1722, Milk Car. B&M milk car #1722 was built by Laconia in 1923 and Thermo-King mechanical refrigeration applied in 1951. It was used in Brookside Farms service for First National Stores, generally between Bellows Falls, Vermont, and Boston, Massachusetts, with service lasting until 1960. Number 1722 was photographed at Bellows Falls, Vermont, on April 19, 1958.

B&M #1878, Milk Car. The Boston & Maine acquired six all-steel milk cars from the Erie Railroad. Originally built by Greenville Car Company in 1937, the B&M numbered the cars #1875 – 1880. Photographed at Charlestown, Massachusetts, on April 19, 1960, B&M #1878 (former Erie #6663) was in H. P. Hood Company milk service. The cars had steam and signal lines for head-end passenger service and rode on four-wheel cast steel trucks. Cars #1875 – 1877 were purchased in September 1953 and #1878 – 1880 in August 1954, all for H. P. Hood milk service at Charlestown.

Boston & Maine Steel Milk Cars

Number	Former	Builder	Date	Notes
1875 – 1880	Erie 6656 6657, 6660, 6663 6680, 6683	Greenville	1936	28 ton capacity
1900 – 1914		GATC	1958	2 door
1915 – 1934		GATC	1957	1 door

7. COMBINES

B&M #2091, Passenger-baggage. B&M's Concord Shops in New Hampshire assembled #2091 in April 1903 of wooden construction, later equipped with a steel underframe. This 66,900 pound car had a 50-seat passenger section and a single door baggage section. Concord Shops scrapped the car in July 1947. Number 2091 was photographed at Rockport, Massachusetts, on July 5, 1936.

B&M #2096, Combine. Boston & Maine combine #2096 was built by the railroad's shop at Concord, New Hampshire, in July 1904. This open platform combination baggage-coach had a wooden body and steel underframe. The 67,500 combine was sixty feet, two inches long over sheathing, seated fifty in the passenger section and had a single door per side baggage section. Riding on four-wheel, drop-equalized trucks, the car still had truss-rods when photographed at the North Station storage yard. In May 1952, the combine became work car #W3210 for just a few years before being destroyed at Billerica Shops in June 1956.

B&M #2115, Combine. The Laconia Car Company built the #2115 – 2120 group of combines in September 1909, measuring sixty-one feet, two inches long over sheathing. Combine #2115 had a light weight of 83,800 pounds and seated forty-six in the coach section. The wooden carbody with truss-rod underframe rode on four-wheel, drop-equalized trucks, and was later equipped with a steel center sill. Combine #2115 was photographed on May 1, 1949.

B&M #2126, Passenger-baggage. Wason Car Company was the builder for non-vestibule passenger-baggage cars #2121 – 2138. The car length was 61' 2" and the light weight of the car about 90,000 pounds. Number 2136 had a seating capacity of 38 in the passenger section, often used as the smoker, and two baggage doors on each side of the baggage section. Billerica Shops scrapped #2126 in December 1953. Boston, North Station, was the photo location for #2126 in May 1937.

PASSENGER CARS OF NEW ENGLAND

B7M #2136, Passenger-baggage. Built by Wason Car Company at the same time as #2126, #2136's design included only a single door on each side of the baggage section. Shipped from Wason in October 1910, #2136 also weighed 91,200 pounds and rode on 4-wheeled drop-equalized friction bearing trucks. Never renumbered, #2136 continued in passenger service until scrapped in December 1953 as the first wave of RDC's started to arrive. B&M #2136 was photographed at Manchester, New Hampshire, on July 17, 1935.

B&M #2149, Passenger-baggage. Wooden combination passenger-baggage card #1999 was built by the Pullman Car Company in May 1907 with vestibules. Each vestibule had outside round-top windows and the car was later equipped with a steel underframe. Measuring 60' 1" long over couplers, #1999 rode on 4-wheel drop-equalized trucks. In June 1932, #1999 was renumbered #2149 and continued in passenger service until scrapped at Billerica Shops in December 1950. The passenger section seated 48 and the baggage section had one sliding door on each side. Stained glass windows were mounted over the double-pane side-glass windows. Number 2149 photograph was taken at Portsmouth, New Hampshire, on August 2, 1936.

B&M #2173, Passenger-baggage. Passenger-baggage car #2173 started as a 74-seat coach #1125 at the Pullman Car Company in May 1896. It was rebuilt by the B&M to a combine in April 1929 with two sliding-side-doors on each side. During World War II, it was rebuilt to caboose #103506, then changed to Mechanical Department car #M3099 in May 1951 for non-revenue service. Destroyed in a fire at Boston, it was authorized for retirement in June 1974, B&M #2173 was placed on film at Greenfield, Massachusetts, on June 3, 1934.

B&M #2392 – 2399 Series. Wason Car Company build the #2392 – 2399 group of wooden baggage and mail cars in August and September 1911. Number 2392 was renumbered to #0578 in 1929 and destroyed by fire in 1937. The second car of the group, #2393, was sold to the Suncook Valley Railroad in 1930, leaving the #2394 – 2399 group in service until the 1949 – 1953 period. One of the group waited at Boston after World War II. The photograph shows the B-end with handbrake, safety appliances and end diaphragm. The postal section included four side windows with storm windows and one side-door.

B&M #3801, Combine BLUE JAY. B&M combine #3801, BLUE JAY, was built by Pullman – Standard at the Osgood-Bradley plant in 1947 under plan 46353. The order included B&M cars #3800 – 3801 and MEC combine #540 – 541. These eighty-five foot cars had a coach seating compartment seating thirty-six, a smoking lounge for eight and an almost thirty-foot long baggage room with two six-foot wide sliding doors, one on each side. The cars rode on 41-NP trucks with a combination of helical and elliptical bolster springs. Cosmetic corrugations were applied over the steel sides above and below the side windows and the road name placed in five and one-half-inch letters centered above the windows on the twenty-five- inch nameplate. Combine #3801 was photographed at North Station, Boston, on May 26, 1951, on a Boston – Portland – Bangor train.

107. PROTECTION OF PASSENGERS

In two or more track territory Express Passenger and Fast Freight trains leaving terminals, entering two or more tracks at junctions, and passing terminals of short-run local passenger trains, will, when practicable, be notified of any overdue Local Passenger Trains moving in the opposite direction. Unless otherwise provided by Division Special Instructions or Bulletin Order, it will be the duty of Train Dispatchers to transmit this notice. This does not relieve enginemen from responsibility in compliance with General Rule 107.

In all cases where passenger trains are cut for crossings or other purposes, and there is liability of passengers boarding or leaving train, conductors and trainmen must see that guard chains or gates are in position to prevent people walking off end of cars.

Outside vestibule doors and platform gates on cars in passenger trains will be kept closed on both sides of both through and local trains, except those gates or doors that it is necessary to use to receive or discharge passengers.

When passenger trains stop at stations, coaches must be kept clear of bridges to avoid liability of injury to passengers. This rule must also be observed at stations where there are other openings not properly protected for the safe delivery of passengers. Trains must in all cases stop to clear such bridge or opening.

Every possible effort must be made by freight enginemen on two or more tracks to avoid getting into station where passenger train is scheduled to stop, on the time of such passenger train, thus preventing passengers from crossing to opposite track to board their train.

In cases where this cannot be anticipated, passenger conductors will not start their train until passengers are given an opportunity to get across to their train.

When two passenger trains on two or more tracks approach a station at the same time the outward train will hold back in entering the station between midnight and 12 noon, and the inward train will hold back between 12 noon and midnight between Boston and Reading, Beverly, Lawrence, Lowell, and Ayer.

Unauthorized and unscheduled stops of any train, either freight or passenger, for the purpose of entraining or detraining persons, either paying passengers or employes, must not be made except in emergency cases where the conductor, feeling that the conditions warrant, instructs that the stop be made.

In no case, and under no conditions, must any arrangement other than for a full and positive stop be made for the purpose of entraining or detraining any passenger, paying or employe, and no stop shall be made except on instructions, or in a real emergency, at any point other than a designated passenger station.

From 1963 B&M Employee Timetable, courtesy TRP.

8. RPO-BAGGAGE CARS

B&M #2337, Baggage-mail. Formerly built by the Fitchburg Railroad in 1883 at their company shops, this baggage-mail car was renumbered 2231 when joining the B&M and later in September 1915 changed to #2337. This non-vestibule car with blind ends measured 58' 9" over couplers and had a light weight of 82,000 pounds. With a reduced need for RPOs, #2337 changed to #W3271 in work train service in September 1941. Scrapping took place at Billerica Shops in December 1953. Under the wire, #2337 was photographed at North Adams, Massachusetts, on February 22, 1937.

B&M #2396, Baggage-mail. Wason Car Company built wooden baggage-mail cars #2392 – 2399 in August and September 1911. With blind ends, the cars measured 61' 1½" long and had a weight of 90,000 pounds. Each car had a single baggage door and a single mail door per side. With the arrival of RDC cars and the reduction in passenger train service, #2396 was scrapped at Billerica Shops in December 1953. In Boston – Troy operation, #2396 was photographed at Troy, New York, on April 19, 1936.

B&M #3181, RPO – Baggage. B&M #3181 was a former troop sleeper rebuilt by the B&M into an RPO – baggage car. A fifteen-foot mail section was built at the A end of the car and a baggage section with single side door built at the B end. By the time of the photograph at North Station in Boston on October 13, 1954, #3181 rode on Chrysler cushioned four-wheel friction-bearing trucks and the car equipped with two-inch steam connectors. Originally built by Pullman – Standard in 1944, #3181 was one of three troop sleepers acquired in 1949 and rebuilt to RPO – mail storage cars #3180 – 3182.

9. BAGGAGE CARS

B&M #2818, Baggage. Wooden baggage cars with blind ends, #2813 – 2853, were built by the Laconia Car Company in 1911 – 1912 for the Boston and Maine. Car #2818 arrived on the B&M in December 1911 with a length of 63' 10" over couplers and after the application of a steel underframe by 1926 had a light weight of 92,500 pounds. With twin double doors on each side, the car rode on four-wheel, drop-equalized trucks. Newly painted, #2818 was photographed at Quincy, Massachusetts, on November 1, 1952, and later, September 1956, destroyed at Billerica Shops.

B&M #2826, Baggage. In service at North Station, Boston, #2826 waited for another load while under steam sometime after 1953. Laconia Car Company built this baggage car in January 1912 with a truss-rod underframe and four-wheel trucks. The car was used on several snow trains before being retired and scrapped in March 1957.

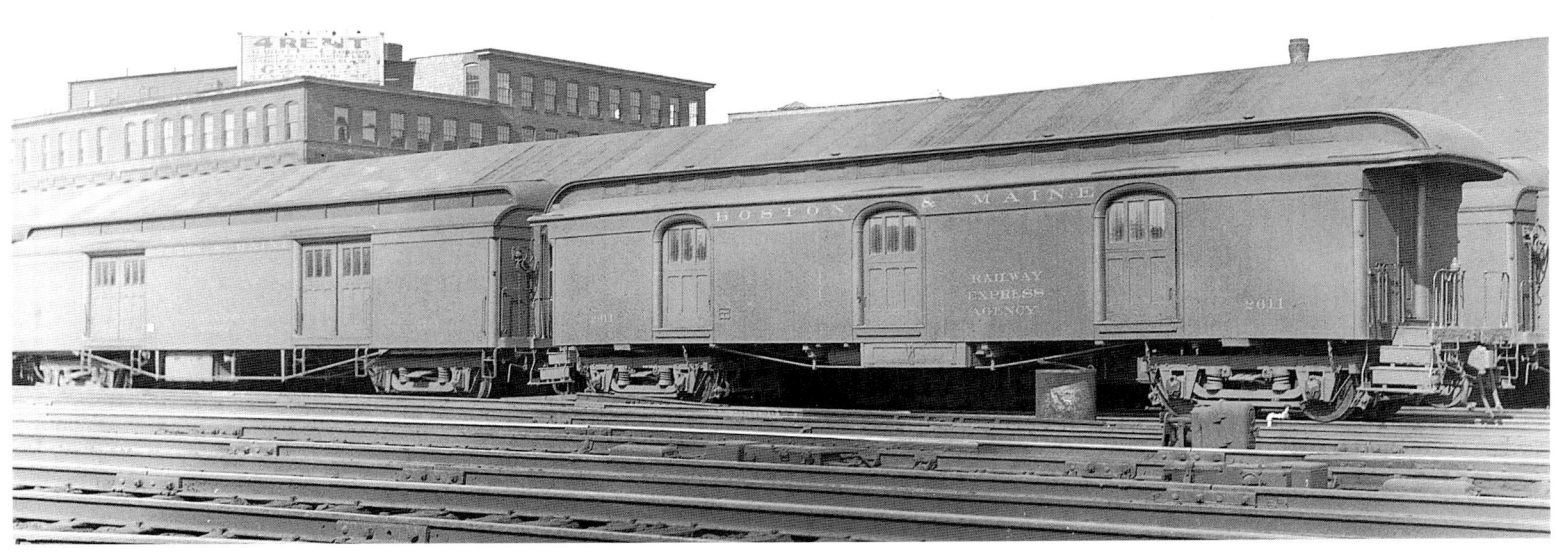

B&M #2611, Baggage. Boston & Maine wooden open-platform baggage car #2611 was built in its Salem, Massachusetts, shops in November 1899. With three baggage doors per side, the truss-rod underframe baggage car rode on four-wheel trucks. Originally built as #74, the car was renumbered 2611 in January 1901 and destroyed at East Deerfield Shops in April 1939. In the passenger storage yard at Springfield, Massachusetts, #2611 was photographed on October 1, 1933.

10. STEEL COACHES

B&M #4557, Coach. Osgood-Bradley Car Company of Worcester built groups of 4500 series coaches in 1922 and 1923. Car #4557 was delivered to the B&M on May 14, 1923, as an 84-seat steel coach. The car measured 80' 1" over buffers and rode on Commonwealth four-wheel drop-equalized trucks. Two toilet rooms were included with washbasins later added. Boston & Maine's standard color scheme was Pullman Green with gold leaf lettering. For intercity service, #4557 later received "bucket" seats and an ice-activated air conditioning system. Number 4557 was sold in June 1959 to the International Railway Equipment Corporation. Rockport, Massachusetts, was the scene for #4457 in April 1938.

B&M #4581, Coach. Osgood-Bradley built in 1931 coaches B&M #4581 – 4584 and MEC #261 – 265 in a joint order. These cars had a seating capacity of sixty-eight in "bucket" type seats, and rode on roller-bearing, four-wheel, drop-equalizer trucks. B&M #4581 builder's photograph was taken at Worcester, Massachusetts, in 1931. This car went to the Maine Central as car #266 in May 1950.

B&M Pacific #3712 with EAST WIND. Boston & Maine Pacific #3712 had backed and coupled to its train at Worcester, Massachusetts, on July 28, 1049. P-4a class #3712 would haul this special six or seven car train from Worcester to Portland over the B&M route. B&M and New Haven as well as the Pennsylvania Railroad supplied passenger equipment for this train, all painted in a silver, black and yellow color scheme, painted each year and back to PRR Tuscan red each fall. Lima built #3712 in December 1934 and it was later renamed the EAST WIND. The first car in the train was a New Haven #5570 – 5589 all-steel baggage car built close by at Osgood-Bradley in 1927 followed by two modernized P-70 coaches.

B&M #4590, Coach. In March 1935, the B&M received delivery of ten "American Flyer" type coaches, #4585 – 4594 from the Osgood-Bradley plant of Pullman-Standard. These 84-seat coaches had men's and women's rooms located at one end and vestibules at both ends. Measuring 84' 6¼" in length over buffers, the carbody had ten double windows and two single windows per side. Each Commonwealth drop-equalizer truck had 5 x 9 friction pounds and 36-inch wheels. Number 4590 was photographed at East Troy, New York, on August 15, 1935, about six months after delivery equipped with early designed roller bearings. Sold to the Long Island Railroad in October 1958, #4590 became LI #7526.

B&M #4601, Coach. B&M second order for "American Flyer" designed coaches came between September and November 1937. Similar to the New Haven "American Flyer" cars, B&M purchased the cars without side skirting and without roller bearings. Like the first order, the cars had 84 seats and Howard luggage racks. Frigidaire air-conditioning units were specified on both orders. Number 4601 was photographed at White River Junction, Vermont, on August 24, 1947. Sold to the Long Island Railroad in July 1959, B&M #4601 became LI #7541.

B&M #4603, Coach. At North Adams, Massachusetts, #4603 waited in train at the passenger station in October 1937. With a working steam heat system and loaded with passengers, this "American Flyer" coach would soon be on the road. The car was only a few weeks old and a member of B&M second group of lightweight coaches #4595 – 4614. These 84-seat coaches continued in service until sold to the Long Island in 1959 with #4603 becoming Long Island #7548 and redesigned for 3 – 2 seating.

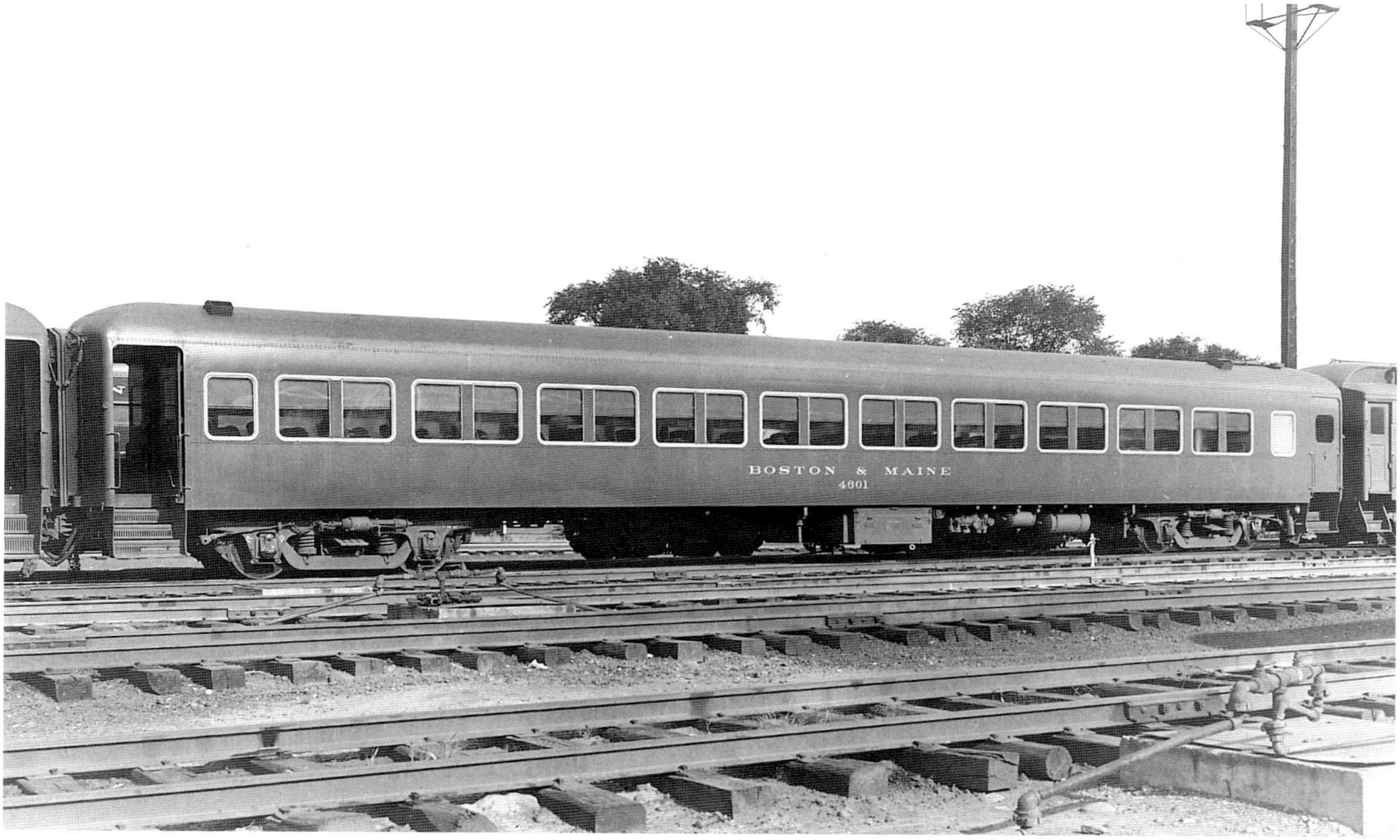
BOSTON & MAINE
4601

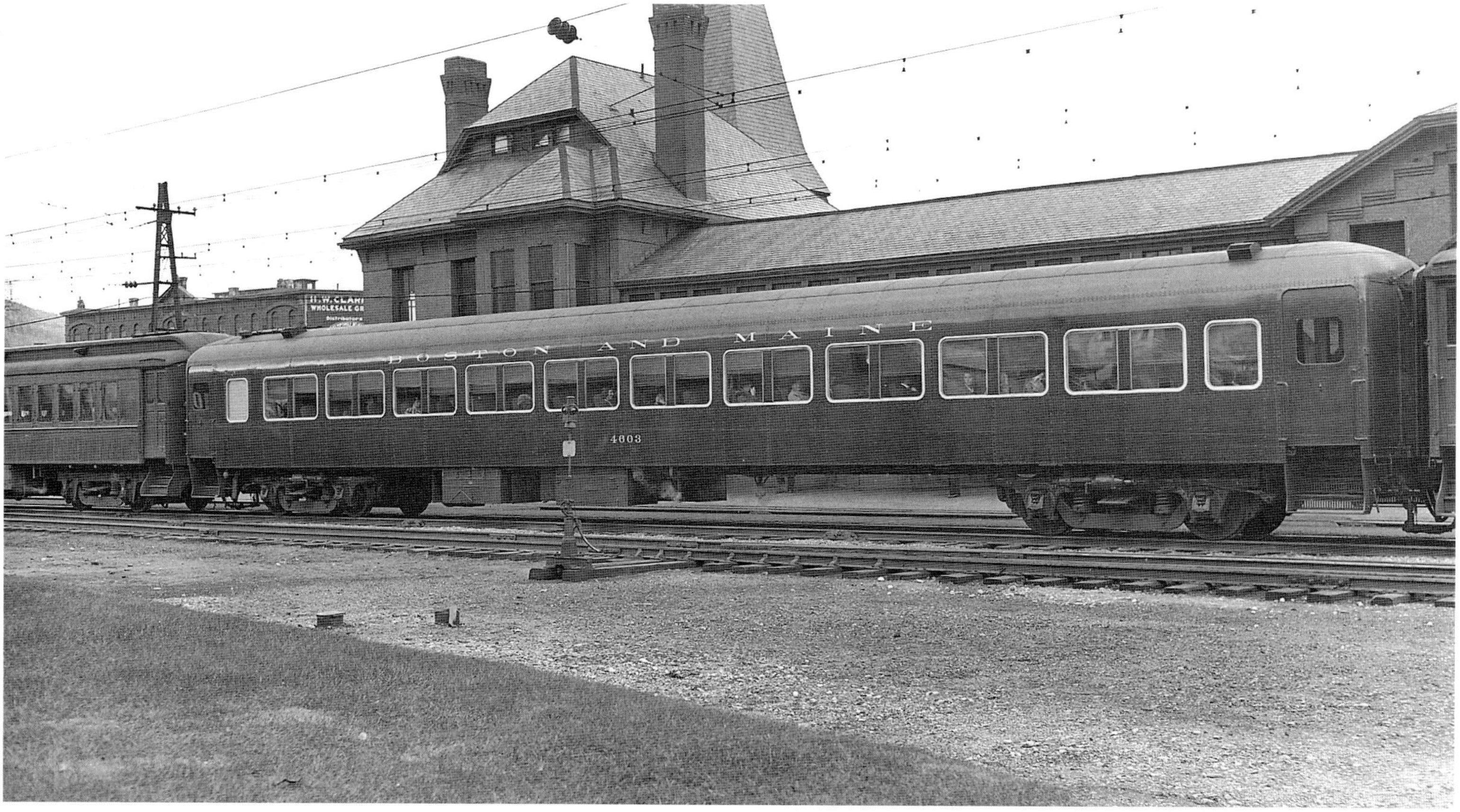
BOSTON AND MAINE
4603

B&M #4801, Coach "ROBIN". In November 1945, jointly the B&M and Maine Central Railroads ordered sixteen coaches from Pullman-Standard for assembly at Osgood-Bradley, Lot W6778, plan W46352. Delivered in June and July 1947, the cars were used on intercity trains between Boston – Portland – Bangor. Each of these coaches had a 56-seat chair section and a 10-seat smoking-lounge. The vestibule end of the car was the B end and the smoking-lounge positioned at the blind or A end of the car. Each car rode on 41-NP trucks and measured 85' over pulling face of couplers. The B&M coaches were numbered 4800 – 4807 with the second car, #4801 named "ROBIN". Opposite the train shed at Bangor Station, #4801 remained on a siding on July 20, 1952.

OPERATION OF TALGO TRAIN

The Talgo-type train, consisting of articulated coaches 100 to 104 inclusive, is powered by Engines 1 and 2. This train is approved for operation over all lines of the Boston and Maine Railroad provided that one of the engines is at each end.

If in an emergency this equipment should have to operate without an engine at each end Conductor must notify train dispatcher who in turn must notify operators of interlocking plants not to change position of switches over which it moves until they know the entire train has passed beyond that interlocking, not depending on model board lights.

If Talgo-type cars are operated on the rear of a train without a locomotive behind these cars, the rear of the train must be protected by manual block, and the note to Rule 99 will not apply.

From 1963 B&M Employee Timetable, courtesy TRP.

B&M Talgo train. After testing on the New Haven, the ACF Talgo train tested on the B&M during the summer of 1955. The B-B trucked locomotive and a three-section coach plus transition section backed out of North Station on September 26, 1955. The end of the rear section had an end cap applied to close off the end-of-train. It would be in December 1957 when FM completed the two Speed Merchant locomotives, #1 and 2, for the Boston & Maine, and the B&M's Talgo train could be delivered, an improved version of these demonstrator coaches.

Volume I Boston & Maine

PAGE 40

PASSENGER CARS OF NEW ENGLAND

11. RDC CARS

B&M #6105, RDC-1. Making a station stop at Greenfield, Massachusetts, on August 6, 1955, was B&M RDC-1 #6105. The B&M ordered the Budd RDC from stock in August 1953, two RDC-1 cars, #6104 and 6105, had been built in June for immediate delivery. Boston and Maine #6105, Budd serial number 5915, operated in that road's passenger service until December 1976 when it was sold to the MBTA as their #6105, sold in 1990 to the Hobo Railroad (Lincoln, New Hampshire).

B&M #6000, Center Section. B&M's three-unit streamlined, stainless-steel Budd-built train #6000 arrived at North Station on February 9, 1935. The second or middle car was fifty-four feet long containing two compartments seating twenty-four and thirty-six. There were three small baggage storage compartments and a linen locker in this unit. One side door on each side was off-set from the center of the car and the trucks at the ends were shared with the two other units of the train. This center section of train #6000 was photographed at the Bangor and Portland train sheds in July 1935, a few months after entering service between Boston and Bangor.

Boston & Maine
Budd RDC Roster 1952-1960

Numbers	Type	Built	Numbers	Type	Built
6100 –6101	RDC-1	1952	6212 – 6213	RDC-2	1956
6102 – 6103	RDC-1	1953	6214	RDC-2	1958
6104 – 6105	RDC-1	1953	6300	RDC-3	1952
6106 – 6148	RDC-1	1955	6301	RDC-3	1953
6149 – 6151	RDC-1	1955	6302	RDC-3	1953
6152 – 6153	RDC-1	1956	6303 – 6306	RDC-3	1958
6154 – 6156	RDC-1	1957	*6900 – 6929	RDC-9	1956
6200 – 6211	RDC-2	1955	*Single Engine		

B&M #6141, RDC-1. Coupled to a Canadian Pacific RDC-2, B&M #6141 stopped at White River Junction on August 8, 1957, when in Boston – Montreal service. Ordered in July 1954, #6141 was one of the #6106 – 6148 group delivered in 1955 to kill the remaining steam-powered commuter trains on the B&M. B&M #6141 became MBTA #6141 in December 1976 and was rebuilt to an unpowered trailer by M-K in July 1982 and re# 413.

12. WORK CARS

B&M #M3037, Work Baggage. This very old work baggage car was used as the tool car in the Boston wreck train. Wooden open platform 1st #M3037 had two baggage doors on each side and drop-equalized trucks. This baggage car was being repainted when photographed at Boston on May 31, 1937.

B&M W3094, Work Combine. Work car #W3094 stopped at Lowell, Massachusetts, in 1950. Originally built as an open platform wooden coach, the car had a truss-rod underframe and four-wheel, drop-equalized trucks. While in non-revenue service, a door was cut in each side at the center of the car.

B&M #W3123, Former coach. B&M work car #W3123 was built by the Osgood-Bradley Car Corporation in June 1887 as a round-roof open-platform coach with a seating capacity of 74. This 64' 6½" long car originally carried a number of 784 when in revenue passenger service and converted to non-revenue service in July 1928 numbered W3123. Working on the west end of the system, #W3123 was finally retired at East Deerfield, Massachusetts, in November 1954. Work coach #W3123 photograph was taken at North Adams, Massachusetts, on February 22, 1937.

B&M #W3159, Work Coach. Boston & Maine work coach #W3159 was in a camp train at North Adams, on February 22, 1937. This open platform wooden car had bunks for the M-of-W crew as well as a small kitchen. The underframe had narrow spaced truss rods, a UC braking system and the carbody rode on four-wheel drop-equalized trucks. Looking at the side, one window was broken and several windows were covered with screens.

B&M #W3204, Former coach. Open platform work coach #W3204 was photographed on the shop track at North Adams, Massachusetts, in October 1937. Number W3204 started out as Fitchburg Railroad coach #159, having been built in the railroad shop in 1892. It was renumbered B&M #746 and remained in passenger service until June 1935 when changed to non-revenue car #W3204. This 63' 9½" long coach weighed 56,600 pounds and seated 72 passengers. It was authorized for retirement in October 1956.

B&M #M3290, Work Coach. B&M #M3290 work coach was used by the Mechanical Department as the kitchen and rider car for the Boston wreck train. The open platform wooden coach rode on four-wheel, drop-equalized trucks and the car had a UC air brake system. This coach's newly painted carbody was supported by four truss rods. Photographed on May 31, 1937, #M3290 was in the North Station yards at Boston, B&M #M3290 was ex#866, ex#554, converted to a work car in October 1934 and scrapped in July 1949.

B&M #W3402, Work Coach. Also located in the camp train at North Adams, on February 22, 1937, was work coach #W3402 in M-of-W service. Coal stoves at both ends heated the car and windows beside the stoves were blanked off. Each side window had an oval pane at the top mounted in a special wood frame. This open-platform former coach rode on four-wheel trucks.

B&M #M3483, Work Coach. Work coach #M3483 was the riding car for the Boston wreck train when photographed at the North Station yard on July 5, 1936. Built by Osgood-Bradley in June 1887, this sixty-four feet, four and one-half inch long open-platform coach was originally Concord and Montreal #183, then renumbered to B&M #781. Seating seventy-seven, the coach was changed to a non-revenue status in September 1926 as #M3483. The car was removed from the wreck train and destroyed at Billerica Shops in December 1946.

B&M #W3772, Work Coach. B&M work coach #W3772 was originally coach #928 built by Laconia Car Company in July 1888. The wooden round roof car was sixty-four feet, five and one-half inches long and had a light weight of 53,700 pounds. In March 1930, coach #928 was changed to M of W #3772. The car was scrapped at North Adams, in July 1947, about ten years after this February 22, 1937, photograph.

B&M #13133, Refrigerator. MDT built the #13100 – 13299 series of refrigerator cars in 1923 for the Boston & Maine. Several cars were later used in passenger car ice service on the B&M. Number 13133 had a fish-belly steel underframe, Andrews trucks, a wooden body and vertical-shaft handbrake when photographed on the B&M at Boston, placed next to an "American Flyer" coach.

INDEX

A
ACF 38
"American Flyer" 3, 36, 48
B
BAR 4
Bellows Falls, Vermont 22
Billerica Shops 7, 9, 10-13, 18, 20, 24, 27, 31, 33, 46
Boston, Massachusetts 3-4, 6-7, 9-10, 13, 18, 20, 22, 24,
.... 27-29, 31, 33, 38, 41-43, 45-46, 48
Brill Company 14
C
Canadian National 4
Clinton, Massachusetts 17
C&O 4
Commonwealth 3, 20, 34, 36
Concord, New Hampshire 23-34, 46
D
DL&W 4
E
East Deerfield Shops 33, 44
East Somerville, Massachusetts 11, 17-18
Electro-Motive Corp 17
Erie Railroad 4, 22
F
Fitchburg Railroad 31
"Flying Yankee" 3
G
Greenville Car Co 22
H
H. P. Hood Co 22
L
Laconia Car Co 3, 10-11, 22, 24, 33, 46
M
Manchester, New Hampshire 27

MBTA 41-42
MEC 3, 28, 34
N
New York Central (NYC) 3-4
New York, New Haven & Hartford 4, 35-36, 38
North Adams, Massachusetts 31, 36, 44-46
North Station 3, 7, 9-10, 12-13, 24, 28,
.... 31, 33, 38, 41, 45-46
O
Osgood-Bradley Car Co 3-4, 12-13, 17, 28, 34-36, 38, 44, 46
P
Pittsburgh & Lake Erie (P&LE) 4
Portland, Maine 2-4, 20, 28, 35, 38, 41
Portsmouth, New Hampshire 14, 27
Pullman Car Co 7-9, 18, 20, 27
Pullman-Standard 3-4, 36, 38
Q
Quincy, Massachusetts 33
R
Reading 4
Reading Highlands 12
Rockport, Massachusetts 8, 23, 34
S
Salem, Massachusett 33
Springfield, Massachusetts 11, 13, 33
T
Talgo 38
Troy, New York 7, 31, 36
W
Wabash 4
Washington, D.C. 2
Wason Car Co 24, 26, 29, 31
Winton 3, 17
Worcester, Massachusetts 2-3, 12, 34-35